-Mapographica-

ART, CULTURE and SPORT

JON RICHARDS *and* ED SIMKINS

WAYLAND

CONTENTS

4–5 GREAT CIVILISATIONS

6–7 ARCHITECTURE

8–9 THE NAME GAME

10–11 FOOD AND DRINK

12–13 READ ALL ABOUT IT

14–15 WEAR IT OUT

16–17 GOING FOR A SONG

18–19 GREAT MINDS

20–21 THE SILVER SCREEN

22–23 CARNIVALS AND FESTIVALS

24–25 A WORLD OF FOOTBALL

26–27 THE OLYMPIC GAMES

28–29 SOCIAL MEDIA

30–31 MAPPING THE WORLD, WEBSITES AND GLOSSARY

32 INDEX

ACKNOWLEDGEMENTS

Published in paperback in 2017 by Wayland
Copyright © Hodder and Stoughton, 2017
All rights reserved
Editor: Julia Adams
Produced for Wayland by Tall Tree Ltd
Designer: Ed Simkins
Editor: Jon Richards

Dewey number: 306.4-dc23
ISBN 978 0 7502 9150 7

Wayland, an imprint of
Hachette Children's Group
Part of Hodder and Stoughton
Carmelite House
50 Victoria Embankment
London EC4Y 0DZ

An Hachette UK Company

www.hachette.co.uk
www.hachettechildrens.co.uk

Printed and bound in China

10 9 8 7 6 5 4 3 2 1

Picture credits can be found on page 32

Our creative — PLANET

If you reduced the world's population to just 100 people, then an 'average' person would not have a college degree, own a computer or use social media. However, they would be able to read and write, and they would be living on more than US$2 a day.

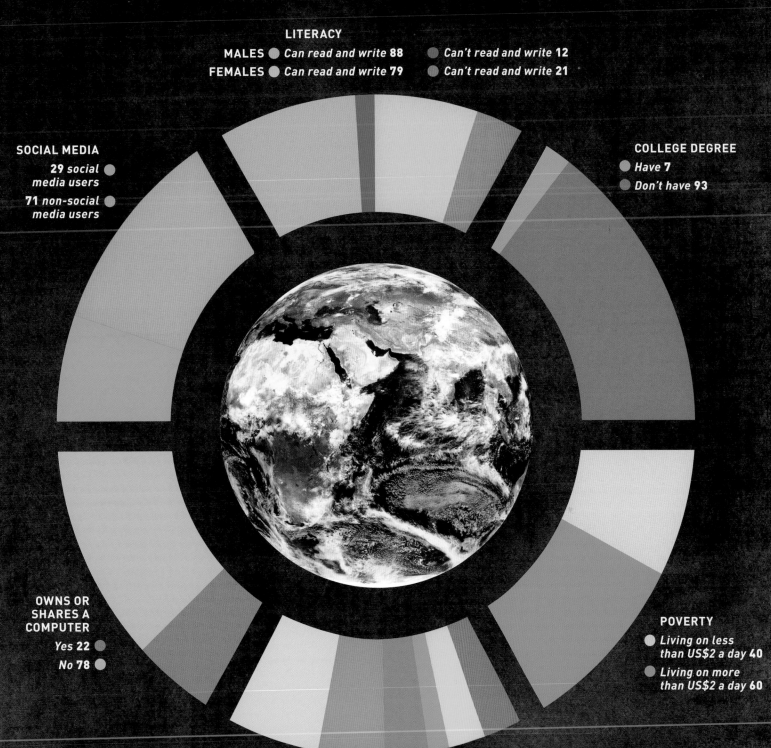

LITERACY
MALES ● *Can read and write* **88**   ● *Can't read and write* **12**
FEMALES ● *Can read and write* **79**   ● *Can't read and write* **21**

SOCIAL MEDIA
29 *social media users* ●
71 *non-social media users* ●

COLLEGE DEGREE
● *Have* **7**
● *Don't have* **93**

OWNS OR SHARES A COMPUTER
Yes **22** ●
No **78** ●

POVERTY
● *Living on less than US$2 a day* **40**
● *Living on more than US$2 a day* **60**

RELIGIONS
● *Christian* **33**   ● *Hindu* **14**   ● *Other religions* **12**
● *Muslim* **22**   ● *Buddhist* **7**   ● *Non-religious* **12**

Great
CIVILISATIONS

Since the first cities were founded more than 10,000 years ago, people have extended the areas they control to create kingdoms and empires. These ruled millions of people and built huge monuments to show their power.

GREAT EMPIRES

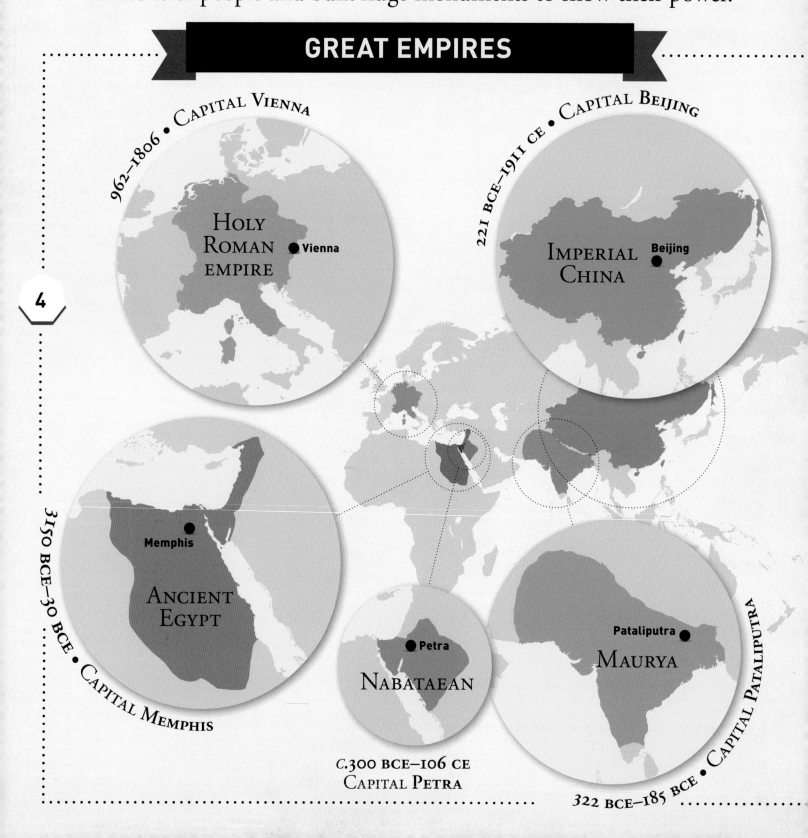

962–1806 • CAPITAL VIENNA

HOLY ROMAN EMPIRE

● Vienna

221 BCE–1911 CE • CAPITAL BEIJING

IMPERIAL CHINA

● Beijing

3150 BCE–30 BCE • CAPITAL MEMPHIS

● Memphis

ANCIENT EGYPT

● Petra

NABATAEAN

C.300 BCE–106 CE
CAPITAL PETRA

Pataliputra ●

MAURYA

CAPITAL PATALIPUTRA

322 BCE–185 BCE

LARGEST EMPIRES

The largest empires covered millions of square kilometres. Although the British empire was the biggest, it was scattered over several continents, making the Mongol empire the largest continuous empire the world has ever seen.

Spanish empire
(1492–1898)
19.4 million sq km

Russian empire
(1723–1917)
22.8 million sq km

British empire
(1597–1997)
33.7 million sq km

Mongol empire
(1206–1368)
33.0 million sq km

Umayyad Caliphate
(661–751 CE)
15.0 million sq km

C.2000 BCE–1697 CE
CAPITAL CHICHEN ITZA

Chichen Itza

MAYA

C.1100–1533 • CAPITAL CUZCO

Cuzco

INCA

Tenochtitlán

AZTEC

C.1300–1521
CAPITAL TENOCHTITLAN

IMPERIAL MONUMENTS

More than 130 pyramids have been discovered in Egypt. The largest is the Pyramid of Khufu, built in 2580 BCE. It weighs as much as 16 Empire State Buildings.

Other great monuments

Teotihuacán
(100 CE) Mexico

Ziggurat of Ur (2000 BCE)
Iraq

Pyramids of Meroe
(700 BCE) Sudan

Chichen Itza
(c.1000 CE) Tikal

ARCHITECTURE

Civilisations around the world have built incredible buildings to act as places of worship, to provide protection or to display their power. Today, architects train for years to design towering skyscrapers and vast shopping centres.

HISTORIC BUILDINGS AROUND THE WORLD

This map shows the locations of some of the most famous buildings and monuments around the world.

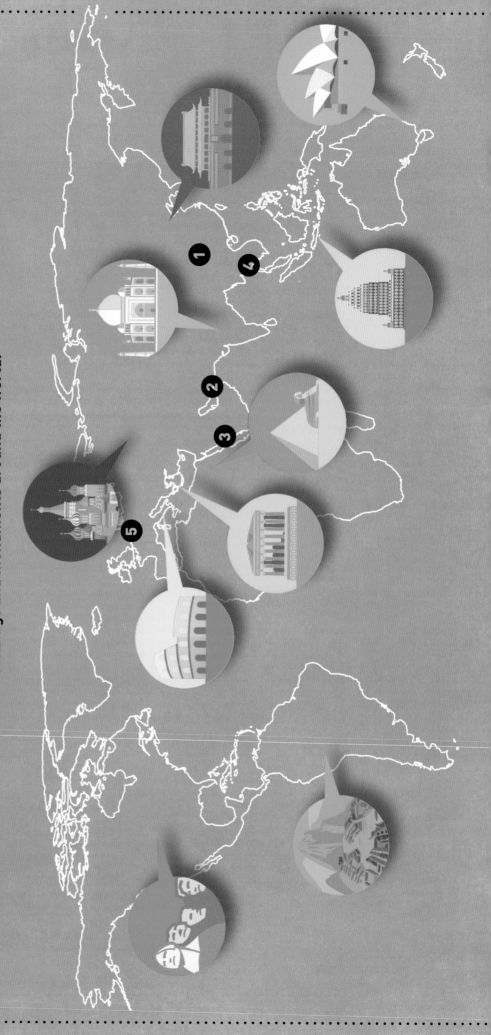

Parthenon

ATHENS, GREECE

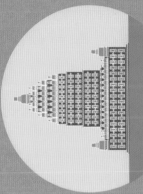

Completed in 432 BCE, the Parthenon is a temple to Athena, the goddess after whom Athens is named. It looks down on the city from the Acropolis Hill.

St Basil's Cathedral

MOSCOW, RUSSIA

Located on Moscow's Red Square, close to the Kremlin, the brightly coloured cathedral was completed in 1561 and is now a museum.

Opera House

SYDNEY, AUSTRALIA

Sydney's performing arts centre sits by the harbour and was opened in 1973. It immediately became the most famous building in Australia.

Prambanan

CENTRAL JAVA, INDONESIA

Prambanan was built in about 850 CE and is the largest Hindu temple complex in Indonesia. It has intricately carved stonework and spires rising to 47 metres.

Taj Mahal

AGRA, INDIA

Shah Jahan ruled over much of India in the mid 17th century. The Taj Mahal, completed in 1654, is a tomb for his third and favourite wife, Mumtaz Mahal.

Forbidden City

BEIJING, CHINA

Completed in 1420 by the Yongle Emperor, the Forbidden City is the world's largest palace complex, with 9,000 rooms and covering an area the size of 20 football pitches.

Colosseum

ROME, ITALY

Built in 80 CE, the Colosseum was the largest amphitheatre in the Roman empire. It could hold more than 50,000 spectators and had huge sails to protect them from the sun's glare.

Mount Rushmore

SOUTH DAKOTA, USA

This huge sculpture, completed in 1939, is carved into the side of a mountain. It features the heads of four US presidents. The heads are about 18 metres tall.

Machu Picchu

CUSCO REGION, PERU

Built around 1450, the city was abandoned soon after the arrival of the Spanish in South America. It remained hidden to the outside world until 1911.

Pyramids

GIZA, EGYPT

Built in about 2500 BCE, the three Great Pyramids at Giza are part of a large burial complex. A colossal sculpture called the Great Sphinx sits in front of them.

LARGEST BUILDINGS BY FLOOR AREA

1. *New Century Global Center* (Chengdu, China) 1,760,000 sq m
2. *Dubai International Airport Terminal 3* (Dubai, UAE) 1,713,000 sq m
3. *Abraj Al-Bait Endowment* (Mecca, Saudi Arabia) 1,575,815 sq m
4. *CentralWorld* (Bangkok, Thailand) 1,024,000 sq m
5. *Aalsmeer Flower Auction* (Aalsmeer, Netherlands) 990,000 sq m

NEW CENTURY GLOBAL CENTER, CHENGDU

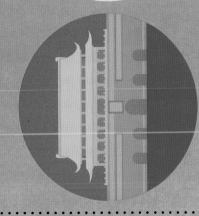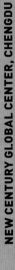

Opened in 2013, the building measures 500 m by 400 m and is about 100 m tall.

It's big enough to fit the Sydney Opera House inside 20 times.

The Name GAME

Around 353,000 babies are born around the world every day. That's more than four babies every second. The names of these babies vary depending on their gender, the country they are born in and their religion.

POPULAR BABY NAMES AROUND THE WORLD

This world map shows some of the most popular children's names in countries around the world, as well as the most common surnames.

Emma | Liam
Olivia | Jacob
Sophia | William
Zoe | Nathan
Mia | Samuel

CANADA

Sophia | Noah
Emma | Liam
Olivia | Jacob
Isabella | Mason
Ava | William

USA

USA
Smith

Fatima | Mohamed
Khadija | Ahmed
Aicha | Mohammed
Malika | Said
Naima | Rachid

Mexico
Martinez

BRAZIL

Brazil
Silva

Sophia | Miguel
Julia | David
Alice | Arthur
Manuela | Gabriel
Isabella | Pedro

KEY

Popular baby names
Girls

Popular baby names
Boys

Country
Name

Most common surnames
The spread of surnames may depend upon a country's history. For example, the spread of the British empire during the 18th and 19th centuries can be seen by the occurrence of British surnames, such as Smith, in English-speaking countries around the globe.

Amelia / Oliver (UK)

Amelia	Oliver
Olivia	Jack
Emily	Harry
Ava	Jacob
Isla	Charlie

UK *Smith*

Ireland *Murphy*

Germany *Müller*

France *Martin*

Italy *Rossi*

Spain *García*

UK

ITALY

A woman from Hartlepool, UK, may have the record for the longest name in the world. Changing her name to raise money for charity, her full name is…

Red – Wacky League – Antlez – Broke the Stereo – Neon Tide – Bring Back Honesty – Coalition – Feedback – Hand of Aces – Keep Going Captain – Let's Pretend – Lost State of Dance – Paper Taxis – Lunar Road – Up! Down! Strange! – All and I – Neon Sheep – Eve Hornby – Faye Bradley – AJ Wilde – Michael Rice – Dion Watts – Matthew Appleyard – John Ashurst – Lauren Swales – Zoe Angus – Jaspreet Singh – Emma Matthews – Nicola Brown – Leanne Pickering – Victoria Davies – Rachel Burnside – Gil Parker – Freya Watson – Alisha Watts – James Pearson – Jacob Sotheran–Darley – Beth Lowery – Jasmine Hewitt – Chloe Gibson – Molly Farquhar – Lewis Murphy – Abbie Coulson – Nick Davies – Harvey Parker – Kyran Williamson – Michael Anderson – Bethany Murray – Sophie Hamilton – Amy Wilkins – Emma Simpson – Liam Wales – Jacob Bartram – Alex Hooks – Rebecca Miller – Caitlin Miller – Sean McCloskey – Dominic Parker – Abbey Sharpe – Elena Larkin – Rebecca Simpson – Nick Dixon – Abbie Farrelly – Liam Grieves – Casey Smith – Liam Downing – Ben Wignall – Elizabeth Hann – Danielle Walker – Lauren Glen – James Johnson – Ben Ervine – Kate Burton – James Hudson – Daniel Mayes – Matthew Kitching – Josh Bennett – Evolution – Dreams.

Sofia	Francesco
Giulia	Alessandro
Giorgia	Andrea
Martina	Lorenzo
Emma	Matthew

Yuina	Hiroto
Hina	Ren
Aoi	Yuuma
Yua	Minato
Yui	Haruto

Sofia	Artem
Maria	Alexander
Daria	Maxim
Arina	Daniel
Anastasia	Michael

Russia *Smimov*

RUSSIA

9

China *Wang*

CHINA

Japan *Sato*

JAPAN

INDIA

Saanvi	Aarav
Aanya	Vivaan
Aadhya	Aditya
Aradhya	Vihaan
Ananya	Arjun

Wang Fang	Zhang Wei
Wang Xiu Ying	Wang Weo
Li Xiu Wing	Li Wei
Li Na	Liu Wei
Zhang Xiu Wing	Li Qiang

MOROCCO

NIGERIA

KENYA

AUSTRALIA

Australia *Smith*

Esther	Emmanuel
Abigail	Michael
Rose	Victor
Stephanie	Peter
Temitope	Kingsley

Faith	John
Winnie	James
Linda	Martin
Sharon	David
Anne	Joseph

Charlotte	Oliver
Olivia	William
Ava	Jack
Emily	Noah
Mia	Jackson

Food and DRINK

People living in rich countries usually eat more than those living in poor nations. The ingredients of different national diets also vary, with some countries eating more meat, while others eat more vegetables.

DAILY DIETS AROUND THE WORLD

This map shows some of the highest and lowest average calorie intakes in countries around the world, as well as how many calories come from different types of food.

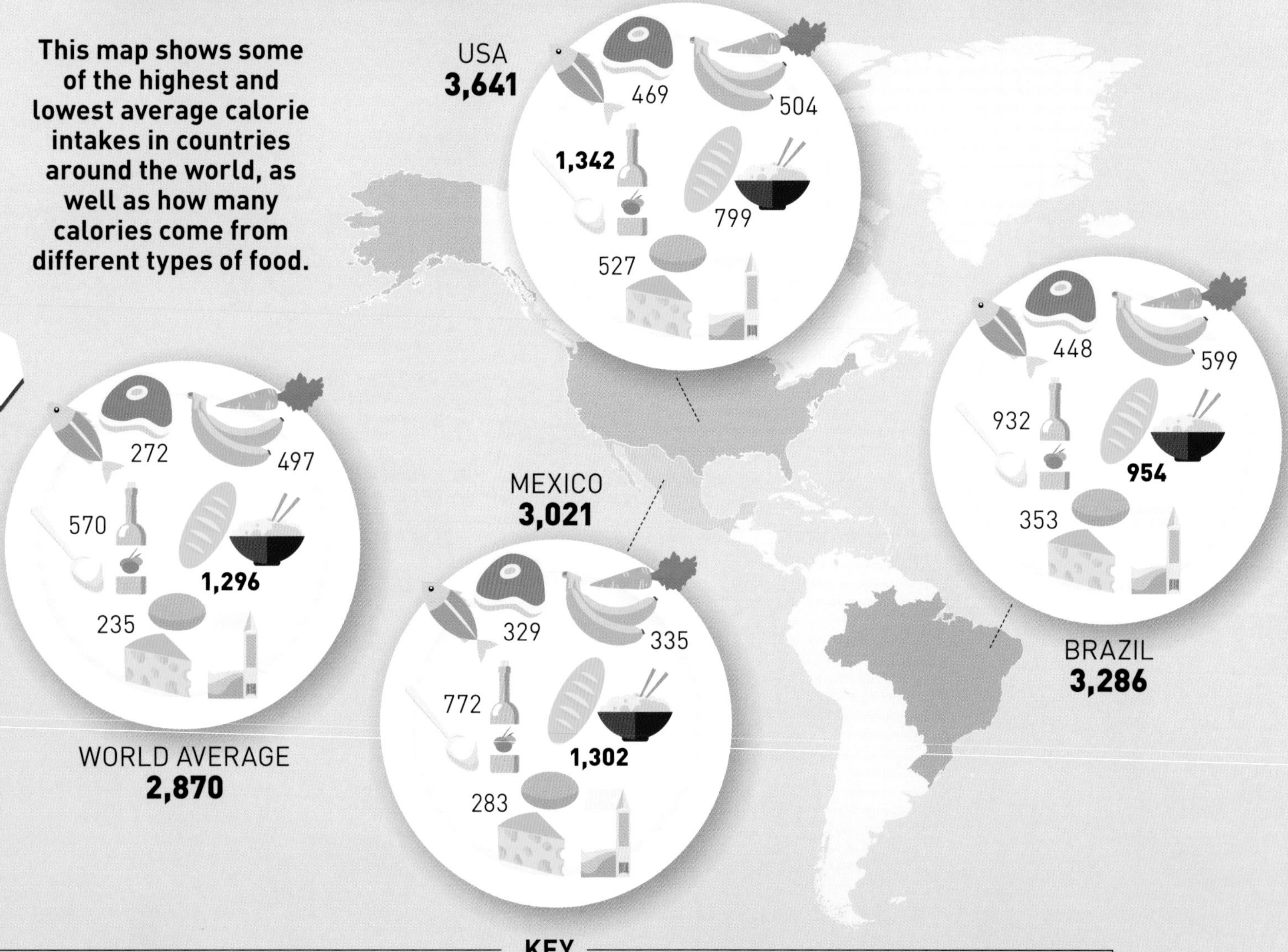

USA
3,641
469
504
1,342
799
527

MEXICO
3,021
329
335
772
1,302
283

BRAZIL
3,286
448
599
932
954
353

WORLD AVERAGE
2,870
272
497
570
1,296
235

KEY

Meat
Meat and fish

Grains
Rice, wheat and corn

Sugar/fat
Sugar and vegetable oil

Dairy/eggs
Eggs, milk and animal fats

Produce
Fruit, vegetables and pulses

Fast food frenzy

In a little over 50 years, McDonald's has increased in size from being a one-restaurant brand to...

36,258 restaurants **in** **119** countries **serving** **69 million** customers every single day.

Fast food outlets worldwide

KFC 18,875

Pizza Hut 14,812

Burger King 12,000

McDonald's 36,258 **Subway** 43,000

Timeline

The first McDonald's restaurant opened in 1948 – it was called the 'McDonald's Bar-B-Q'.

The first franchise McDonald's opened in 1953.

1958 **34** restaurants	1965 **700**	1988 **10,000**	2005 **30,766**
1959 **100**	1968 **1,000**	1996 **20,000**	2009 **32,478**
1963 **500**	1978 **5,000**	1997 **23,000**	2014 **36,258**

489   655
869   **899**
501

UK
3,413

353   588
801   **1,164**
452

RUSSIA
3,358

509   605
338   **1,451**
170

CHINA
3,073

11

97   451
206   **1,318**
31

NORTH KOREA
2,103

122   89
419   **651**
414

SOMALIA
1,695

29   366
471   **1,394**
198

INDIA
2,458

553   516
985   708
505

AUSTRALIA
3,267

Read all — ABOUT IT

More than one million different books are published every year in every language on the planet. While China and the USA publish the most titles, more are released per head of population in the UK than anywhere else, with 2,875 titles published per one million people.

PUBLISHING AROUND THE WORLD

This map shows the countries with the largest publishing markets and how much they earn each year, as well as some of the biggest-selling authors of all time and the number of books they have sold.

— NEW TITLES PUBLISHED BY COUNTRY —

CHINA
444,000

RUSSIA
101,981

JAPAN **77,910**
SPAIN **76,434**
FRANCE **66,527**
ITALY **61,100**
TURKEY **42,626**
TAIWAN **42,118**

UNITED STATES
304,912

GERMANY
93,600

UNITED KINGDOM
184,000

INDIA
82,537

USA
27,400 million euros

RUSSIA
Leo Tolstoy
413 million

SWEDEN
Astrid Lindgren
145 million

CHINA
Jin Yong
300 million

JAPAN
Jirō Akagawa
300 million

Japan
5,409
million euros

China
15,342
million euros

Germany
9,536
million euros

France
4,401
million euros

ZAMBIA
Wilbur Smith
120 million

SPAIN
Corin Tellado
400 million

UNITED KINGDOM
William Shakespeare
4 billion

FRANCE
Georges Simenon
700 million

BRAZIL
Paulo Coelho
140 million

USA
Danielle Steel
800 million

Worldwide — entertainment media turnover

Book publishing
US$151 billion

Magazines
US$107 billion

Music
US$50 billion

Video games
US$63 billion

Movies & entertainment
US$133 billion

The 20 largest publishing markets account for about **84%** **of the total spending on books** (95,609 million euros out of 114,000 million euros)

KEY

Five biggest publishing markets
in millions of euros per year

COUNTRY
Author name
000 million

Bestselling authors
from around the world and the estimated total sales of their books

Wear it OUT

High fashion means big business. However, while most of the clothes we wear are made in some of the poorest countries, the money from sales flows to rich clothing companies who are based in the wealthiest nations.

WORLD'S MOST VALUABLE FASHION BRANDS

This map shows the value of the world's richest clothing brands and where they are located.

Ralph Lauren
USA
US$4.9 billion

Gap
USA
US$4.1 billion

Burberry
UK
US$5.6 billion

Tiffany
USA
US$5.9 billion

Nike
USA
US$19.8 billion

Louis Vuitton
France
US$22.5 billion

Chanel
France
US$7 billion

Hermès
France
US$9 billion

Cartier
France
US$7.4 billion

Zara
Spain
US$12.1 billion

FAIR PAY?

The Asia Floor Wage Alliance calculates what should be the minimum wage in countries that produce most of the world's clothes (bottom figure in euros) and compares it to the current minimum wage (top figure in euros):

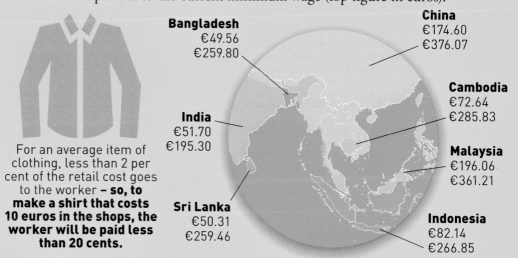

Bangladesh
€49.56
€259.80

China
€174.60
€376.07

India
€51.70
€195.30

Cambodia
€72.64
€285.83

Malaysia
€196.06
€361.21

Sri Lanka
€50.31
€259.46

Indonesia
€82.14
€266.85

For an average item of clothing, less than 2 per cent of the retail cost goes to the worker – **so, to make a shirt that costs 10 euros in the shops, the worker will be paid less than 20 cents.**

H&M
Sweden
US$21 billion

Hugo Boss
Germany
US$4.1 billion

Adidas
Germany
US$7.4 billion

Prada
Italy
US$6 billion

Gucci
Italy
US$10.4 billion

Top 10 COTTON PRODUCING — nations —
(tonnes per year)

China 6,967,000
India 6,641,000
USA 2,811,000
Pakistan 2,068,000
Brazil 1,633,000
Uzbekistan 904,000
Australia 893,000
Turkey 501,000
Turkmenistan 327,000
Greece 298,000

Every year, China produces the same weight in cotton as 35,000 blue whales.

Going for — A SONG

While music sales figures have stayed the same in recent years, how that music is sold has changed dramatically. Today, nearly half of all music earnings comes from digital formats, including downloads and streaming.

MUSIC SALES AND FESTIVALS

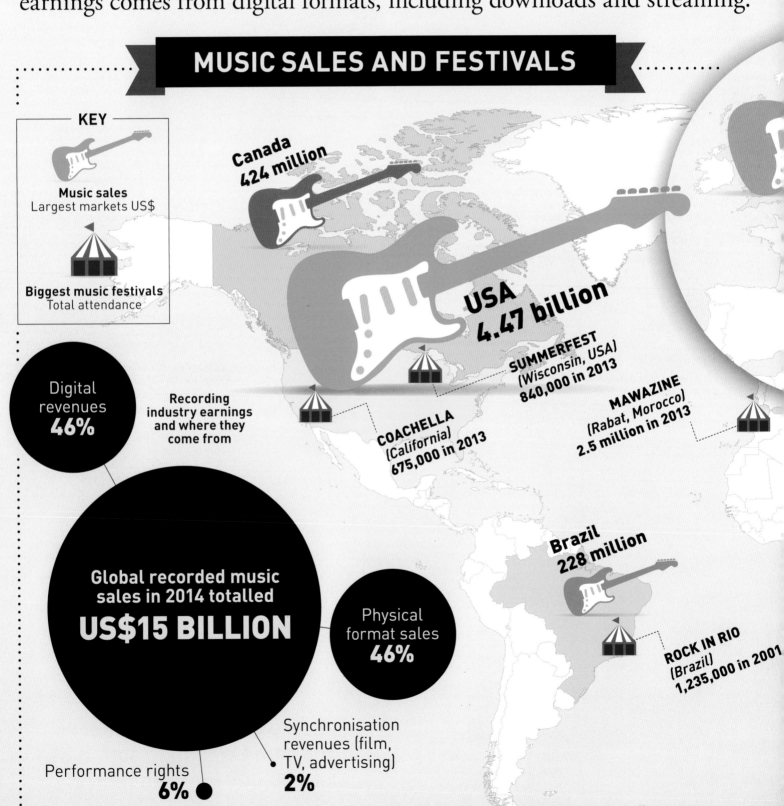

KEY

Music sales
Largest markets US$

Biggest music festivals
Total attendance

Canada
424 million

USA
4.47 billion

Recording industry earnings and where they come from

Digital revenues
46%

Global recorded music sales in 2014 totalled
US$15 BILLION

Physical format sales
46%

Performance rights
6%

Synchronisation revenues (film, TV, advertising)
2%

SUMMERFEST
(Wisconsin, USA)
840,000 in 2013

COACHELLA
(California)
675,000 in 2013

MAWAZINE
(Rabat, Morocco)
2.5 million in 2013

Brazil
228 million

ROCK IN RIO
(Brazil)
1,235,000 in 2001

Streaming earnings

Listening to tracks on the internet without downloading them is known as streaming. Over the last 10 years, this source of revenue has increased dramatically to more than 20 per cent of all music industry earnings.

2007 **3%**   2008 **4%**   2009 **5%**   2010 **7%**   2011 **9%**   2012 **15%**   2013 **21%**

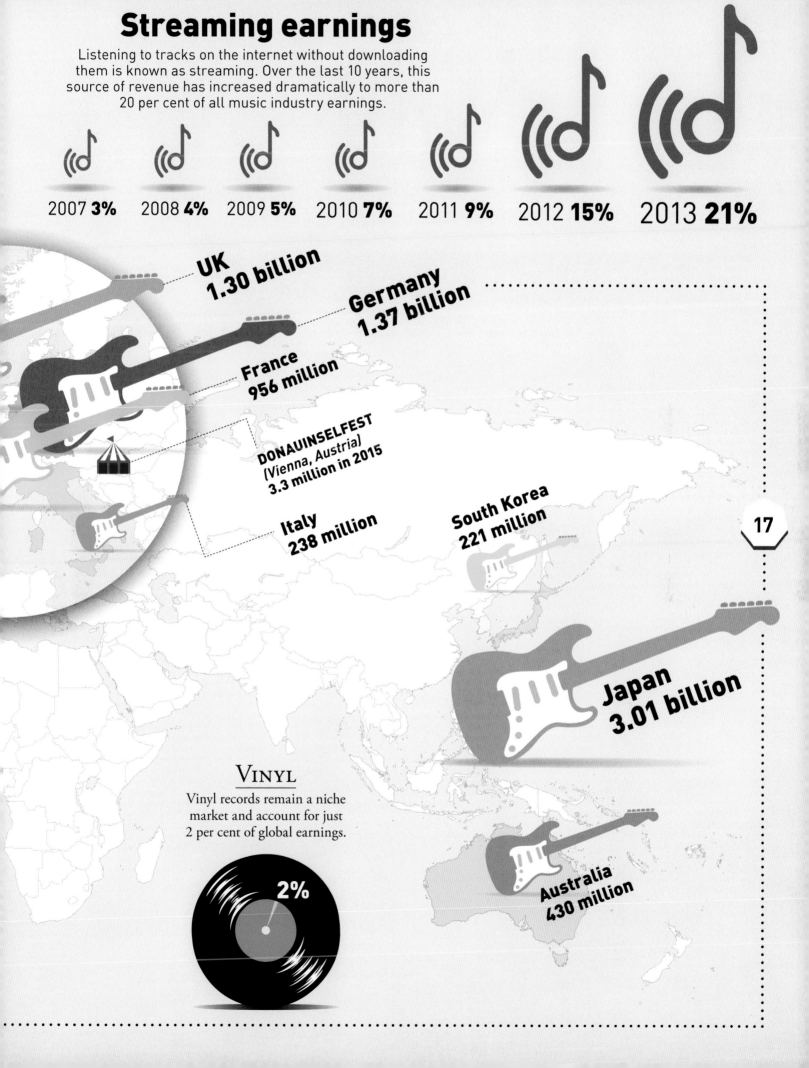

UK
1.30 billion

Germany
1.37 billion

France
956 million

DONAUINSELFEST
(Vienna, Austria)
3.3 million in 2015

Italy
238 million

South Korea
221 million

Japan
3.01 billion

VINYL

Vinyl records remain a niche market and account for just 2 per cent of global earnings.

2%

Australia
430 million

Great MINDS

The amount a country invests in its education system is often reflected in its success in science and industry. However, people living in some of the poorest regions in the world usually have access to the least education.

SPENDING ON EDUCATION

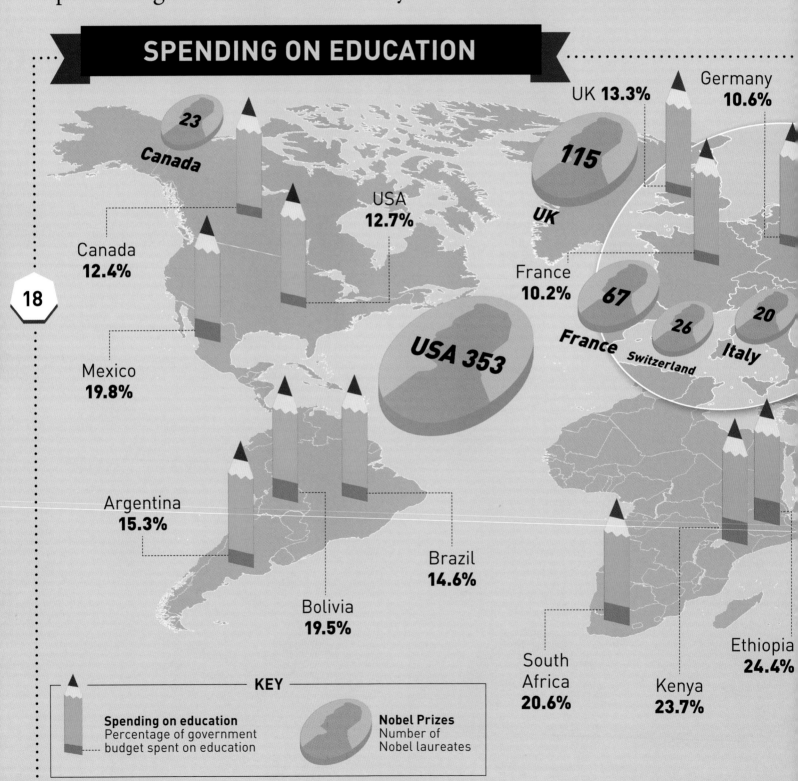

23
Canada

**Canada
12.4%**

**Mexico
19.8%**

USA
12.7%

UK **13.3%**

Germany
10.6%

115
UK

France
10.2%

67
France

26
Switzerland

20
Italy

USA 353

**Argentina
15.3%**

**Bolivia
19.5%**

**Brazil
14.6%**

**South
Africa
20.6%**

**Kenya
23.7%**

**Ethiopia
24.4%**

KEY

Spending on education
Percentage of government
budget spent on education

Nobel Prizes
Number of
Nobel laureates

Teacher conditions

Wealthier countries, such as the USA and Finland, spend more on education so they usually have more teachers available than poorer countries, such as Bangladesh.

Number of students per teacher in secondary education

Central African Republic
68.1

Bangladesh
32.2

Dominican Republic
29.2

USA
14.7

China
14.5

France
12.8

Finland
9.3

Cayman Islands
5.3

NOBEL PRIZE

Created by Swedish engineer and inventor Alfred Nobel, the Nobel Prize is awarded to people for outstanding achievements in the arts, science and politics. Winners of a Nobel Prize are called laureates.

Sweden 30

102

Germany

28
Russia

22
Japan

Japan
9.5%

India
11.3%

Australia
13.5%

Around the world,
61 MILLION
children of primary school age are out of school.

250 MILLION
children cannot read, write or count well.

775 MILLION
adults are illiterate (500 million of these are women).

BUT

Investing in education can improve a whole country's economic situation

US$1 = **US$10**

invested in education and skills

in economic growth

ALFR· NOBEL

NAT· MDCCC XXXIII OB· MDCCC XCVI

The Silver SCREEN

The production and screening of movies is a major global business, with the biggest blockbusters earning more than US$1 billion. Today, the industry stretches far beyond its traditional home of Hollywood.

NUMBER OF FEATURE FILMS PRODUCED

This map shows how many movies are made in countries around the world and the range of languages they are made in.

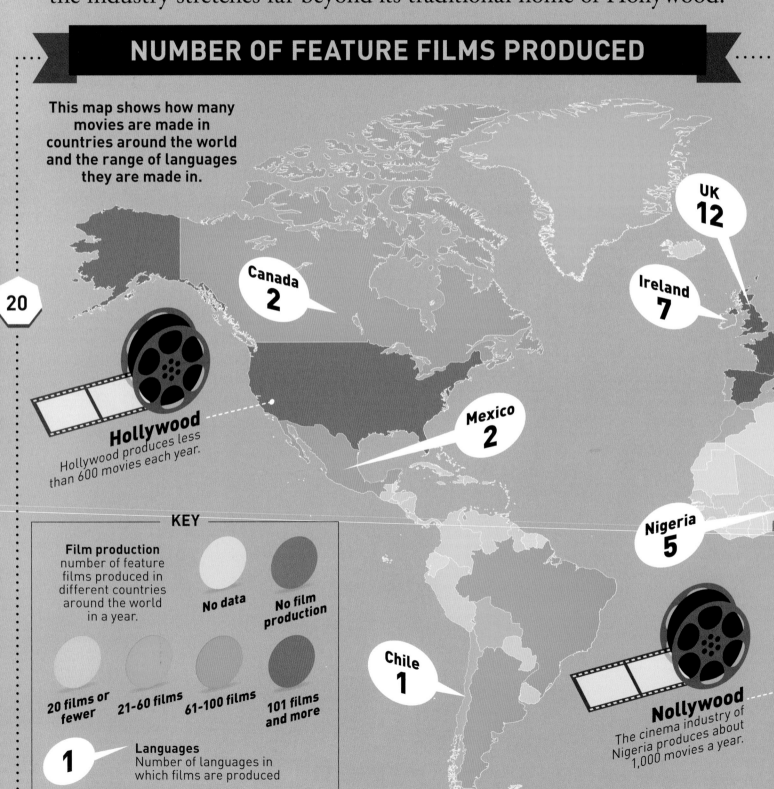

20

Canada
2

UK
12

Ireland
7

Hollywood
Hollywood produces less than 600 movies each year.

Mexico
2

Nigeria
5

Chile
1

Nollywood
The cinema industry of Nigeria produces about 1,000 movies a year.

KEY

Film production
number of feature films produced in different countries around the world in a year.

No data

No film production

20 films or fewer

21-60 films

61-100 films

101 films and more

1 **Languages**
Number of languages in which films are produced

CINEMA ADMISSIONS

While it only has the second-highest level of cinema admissions, the USA has the greatest share of global cinema earnings, taking more than US$10 billion a year, or about 30 per cent of the world's total.

Annual cinema admissions by country

India TICKET ADMIT **2.9 billion**

USA TICKET ADMIT **1.4 billion**

China TICKET ADMIT **264 million**

France TICKET ADMIT **201 million**

Mexico TICKET ADMIT **178 million**

Japan TICKET ADMIT **169 million**

UK TICKET ADMIT **173 million**

South Korea 157 million

Germany 136 million

Russia 132 million

Finland **5**

Turkey **7**

Egypt **1**

South Africa **4**

India **21+**

CHINESE FILM MARKET

The Chinese film market increased by **34%** in 2014, earning **US$4.8bn**.

In contrast, the global market rose by just 1% during the same period.

The country is planning to build 25,000 cinema screens by 2020.

Bollywood
The Indian film industry makes more than 1,200 movies every year.

Carnivals and FESTIVALS

Every year, people gather together in huge celebrations. The largest of these celebrations are for religious reasons and may involve people making special journeys, called pilgrimages, to places they believe to be holy.

THE WORLD'S BIGGEST FESTIVALS

The word 'carnival' is thought to come from the Latin phrase *carne vale*, which means 'goodbye meat'. It refers to the last chance for Christians to eat meat before the fasting period of Lent. Many carnivals today are still held before Lent, while others, such as those in London and Toronto, are held later in the year and are celebrations of other cultures.

Mecca

Haridwar
Allahabad

Manila

Tongi

Ujjain

Nashik

Rio de
Janeiro

LARGEST RELIGIOUS GATHERINGS

WORLD YOUTH DAY
Roman Catholic youth festival held every two to three years.
In 2013, 3.7 million attended in Rio de Janeiro, Brazil.

HAJJ
Annual Islamic pilgrimage to Mecca in Saudi Arabia.
3.2 million in 2012.

KUMBH MELA
Hindu pilgrimage held every three years in the Indian cities of Haridwar, Allahabad, Nashik and Ujjain.
Attended by 100 million.

BISHWA IJTEMA
Annual gathering of the Tablighi Jamaat Islamic movement at Tongi in Bangladesh
Attended by 3 million people.

POPE FRANCIS
On 18 January 2015, the Eucharistic Celebration of his five-day Philippine tour was held in Manila.
Attended by an estimated 6–7 million people.

Mardi Gras
New Orleans, USA
Shrove Tuesday
1,200,000

Carnevale
Venice, Italy
Shrove Tuesday
30,000

Carnival
Port of Spain, Trinidad and Tobago
Sunday before Ash Wednesday
300,000

Carnival
Notting Hill, London, UK
Last weekend in August
1,600,000

Carnaval
Tenerife, Spain
Shrove Tuesday
250,000

Karneval
Cologne, Germany
Rosenmontag
1,000,000

Carnival
Rio de Janeiro, Brazil
Friday before Ash Wednesday
2,000,000

Intruz
Goa, India
Saturday before Ash Wednesday
200,000

Carnival
Barranquilla, Colombia
Saturday before Ash Wednesday
1,000,000

Caribana
Toronto, Canada
First weekend in August
1,300,000

A World of FOOTBALL

Football is the world's most popular sport, with approximately 250 million players, amateur and professional, and 1.3 billion followers in more than 200 countries.

THE BEAUTIFUL GAME

This map shows the countries with the most football players, as well as the locations of the world's richest clubs and largest stadiums.

Countries with the greatest number of football clubs

England 42,490 clubs

Brazil 29,208 clubs

Germany 26,837 clubs

France 20,062 clubs

Spain 18,190 clubs

Italy 16,697 clubs

UNITED STATES The Rose Bowl, Pasadena **92,542**

USA 24,472,778 players

MEXICO Estadio Azteca, Mexico City **105,500**

ENGLAND Wembley Stadium, London **90,000**

SPAIN Camp Nou, Barcelona **99,786**

ALGERIA Stade 5 Juillet 1962, Algiers **85,000**

Brazil 13,197,733 players

KEY

Players Five countries with the highest number of professional and amateur players

Richest World's richest football clubs (total worth)

Stadiums The largest stadiums and their capacity

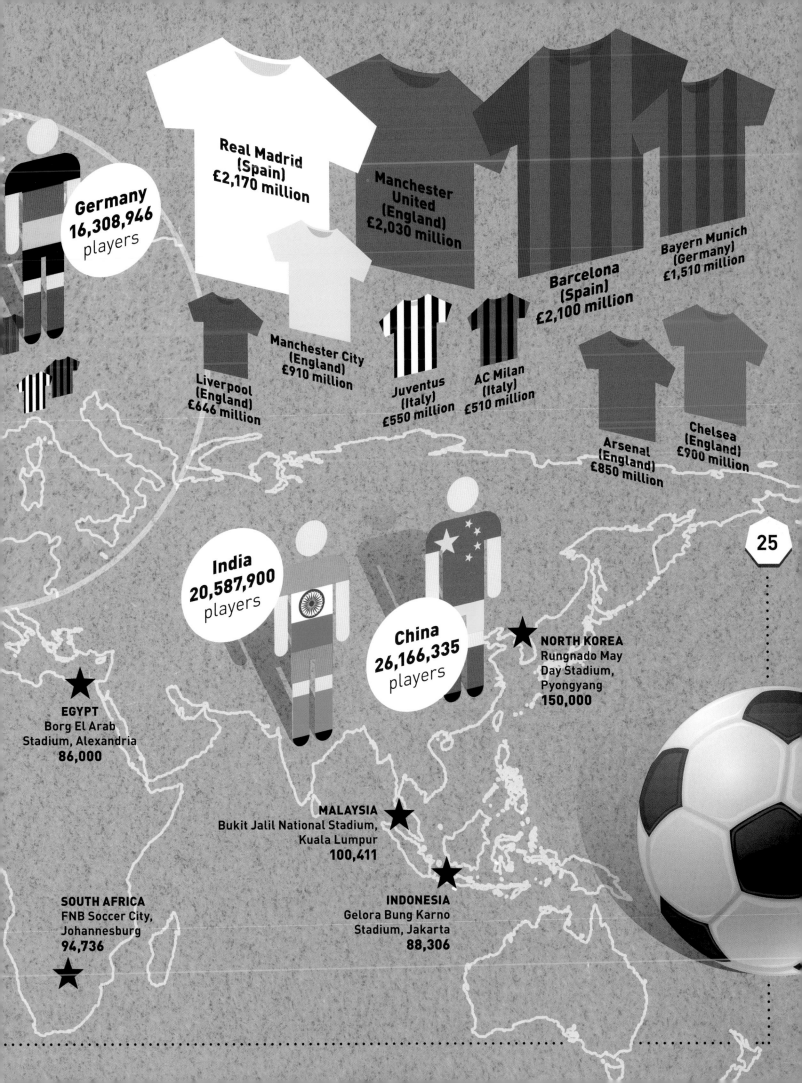

Germany
16,308,946
players

Real Madrid
(Spain)
£2,170 million

Manchester United (England)
£2,030 million

Barcelona (Spain)
£2,100 million

Bayern Munich (Germany)
£1,510 million

Manchester City (England)
£910 million

Liverpool (England)
£646 million

Juventus (Italy)
£550 million

AC Milan (Italy)
£510 million

Arsenal (England)
£850 million

Chelsea (England)
£900 million

India
20,587,900
players

China
26,166,335
players

NORTH KOREA
Rungnado May
Day Stadium,
Pyongyang
150,000

EGYPT
Borg El Arab
Stadium, Alexandria
86,000

MALAYSIA
Bukit Jalil National Stadium,
Kuala Lumpur
100,411

INDONESIA
Gelora Bung Karno
Stadium, Jakarta
88,306

SOUTH AFRICA
FNB Soccer City,
Johannesburg
94,736

The Olympic GAMES

Every four years, thousands of athletes gather to compete in the Summer and Winter Olympic games. So far, the USA has won the most bronze, silver and gold medals at the Summer Olympics with a total of 2,400.

SUMMER AND WINTER MEDALS

This world map shows how successful countries around the world have been at both the Summer and Winter Olympics. It also locates the host cities for both games.

NORWAY 118

1994
1952

GREAT BRITAIN 10 236

1908
1948
2012   1928
        1920
1936
1900   1936   1972
        1928   1964
        1948   1976
    1924   1992   1956
    1968   2006
1992   1960
1984

CANADA 63 59

2010   1988
2002
1960   **USA** 96 976
1996   1904
1932
1984
1968

1976
1932
1980

FRANCE 202

JAMAICA 17

ITALY 198

BRAZIL 23

2016

URUGUAY 2

KEY

Summer gold medals
from selected countries around the world

Winter gold medals
from selected countries around the world

Host Cities
Summer Olympics

Host Cities
Winter Olympics

Greece, **Athens** 1896	Mexico, **Mexico City** 1968
France, **Paris** 1900	Germany, **Munich** 1972
USA, **St Louis** 1904	Canada, **Montreal** 1976
UK, **London** 1908	Soviet Union, **Moscow** 1980
Sweden, **Stockholm** 1912	USA, **Los Angeles** 1984
Belgium, **Antwerp** 1920	South Korea, **Seoul** 1988
France, **Paris** 1924	Spain, **Barcelona** 1992
Netherlands, **Amsterdam** 1928	USA, **Atlanta** 1996
USA, **Los Angeles** 1932	Australia, **Sydney** 2000
Germany, **Berlin** 1936	Greece, **Athens** 2004
UK, **London** 1948	China, **Beijing** 2008
Finland, **Helsinki** 1952	UK, **London** 2012
Australia, **Melbourne** 1956	Brazil, **Rio de Janeiro** 2016
Italy, **Rome** 1960	Japan, **Tokyo** 2020
Japan, **Tokyo** 1964	

France, **Chamonix** 1924	Canada, **Calgary** 1988
Switzerland, **St Moritz** 1928	France, **Albertville** 1992
USA, **Lake Placid** 1932	Norway, **Lillehammer** 1994
Germany, **Garmisch-Partenkirchen** 1936	Japan, **Nagano** 1998
Switzerland, **St Moritz** 1948	USA, **Salt Lake City** 2002
Norway, **Oslo** 1952	Italy, **Turin** 2006
Italy, **Cortina d'Ampezzo** 1956	Canada, **Vancouver** 2010
USA, **Squaw Valley** 1960	Russia, **Sochi** 2014
Austria, **Innsbruck** 1964	South Korea, **Pyeongchang** 2018
France, **Grenoble** 1968	
Japan, **Sapporo** 1972	
Austria, **Innsbruck** 1976	
USA, **Lake Placid** 1980	
Yugoslavia, **Sarajevo** 1984	

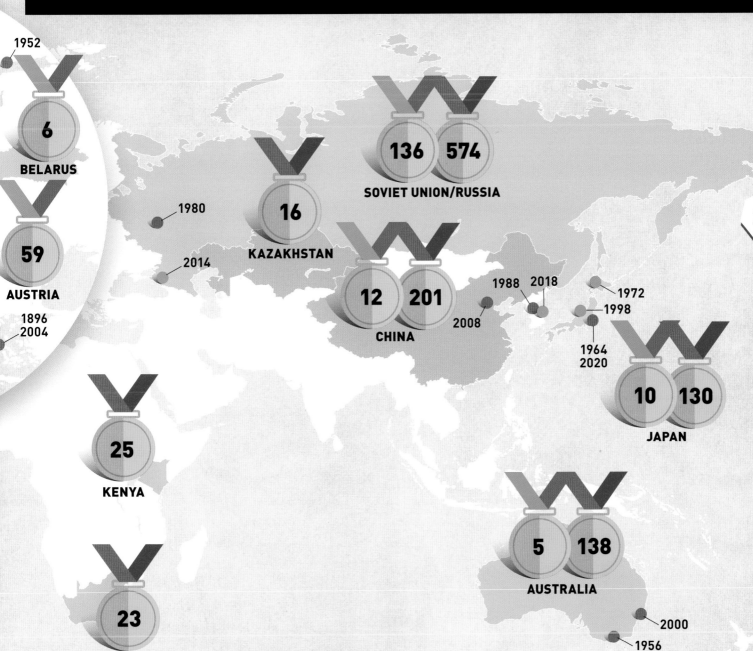

1952

6
BELARUS

136 **574**
SOVIET UNION/RUSSIA

1980

16
KAZAKHSTAN

59
AUSTRIA

2014

1896
2004

12 **201**
CHINA

2008

1988 2018

1972
1998

1964
2020

10 **130**
JAPAN

25
KENYA

5 **138**
AUSTRALIA

2000

1956

23
SOUTH AFRICA

Social MEDIA

Social media allows people to chat and share images with others all over the world. However, no single social network is yet fully global. Russian and Chinese speakers, for example, use large local networks of their own.

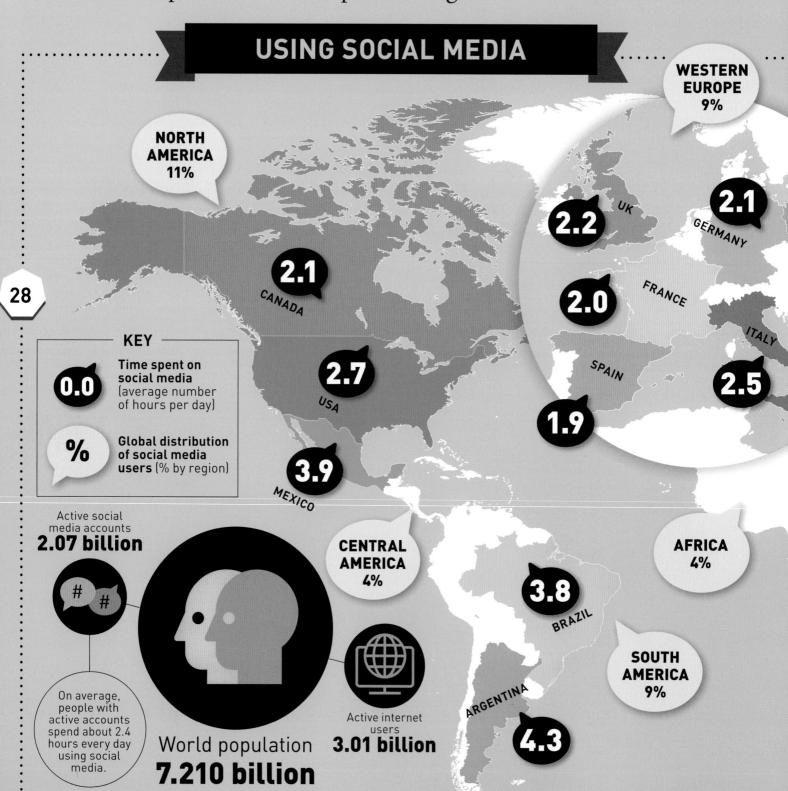

USING SOCIAL MEDIA

WESTERN EUROPE 9%

NORTH AMERICA 11%

UK **2.2**

GERMANY **2.1**

FRANCE **2.0**

ITALY **2.5**

SPAIN **1.9**

CANADA **2.1**

USA **2.7**

MEXICO **3.9**

KEY

0.0 Time spent on social media (average number of hours per day)

% Global distribution of social media users (% by region)

CENTRAL AMERICA 4%

AFRICA 4%

BRAZIL **3.8**

SOUTH AMERICA 9%

ARGENTINA **4.3**

Active social media accounts **2.07 billion**

On average, people with active accounts spend about 2.4 hours every day using social media.

World population **7.210 billion**

Active internet users **3.01 billion**

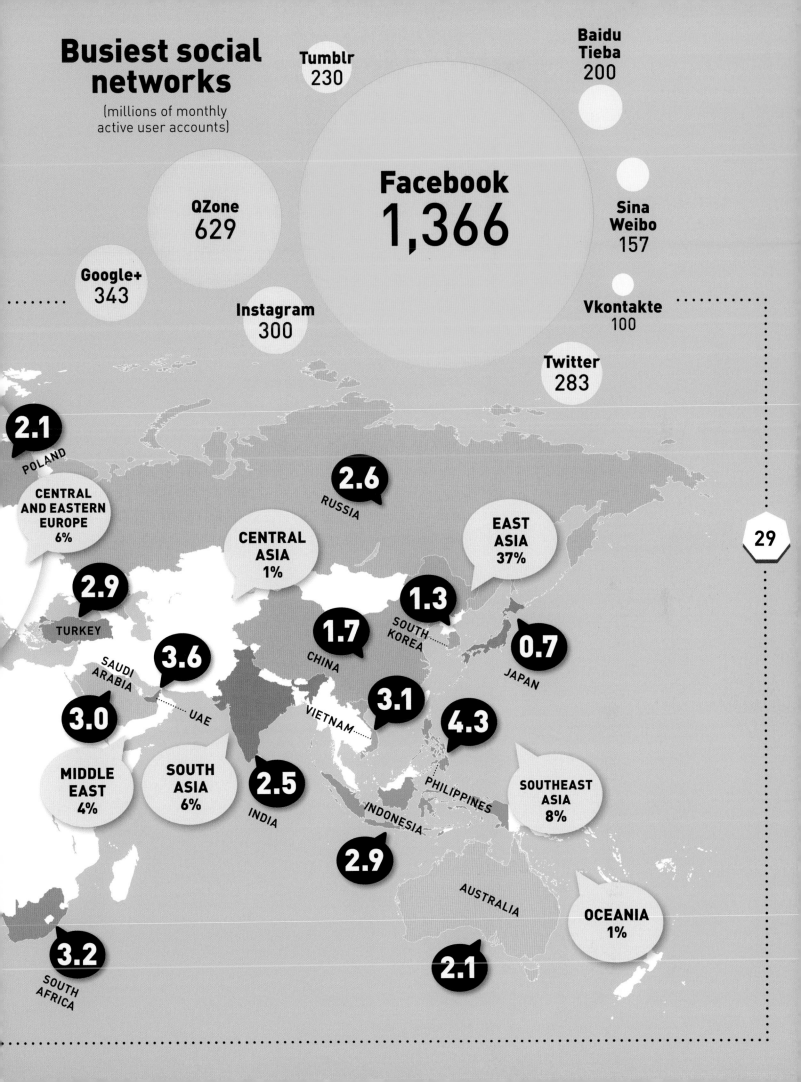

Mapping the
WORLD

The maps in this book are two-dimensional representations of our ball-shaped world. Maps allow us to display a huge range of information, including the size of the countries and where people live.

PROJECTIONS

Converting the three-dimensional world into a two-dimensional map can produce different views, called projections. These projections can show different areas of the Earth.

GLOBE
Earth is shaped like a ball, with the landmasses wrapped around it.

CURVED
Some maps show parts of the world as they would appear on this ball.

FLAT
Maps of the whole world show the landmasses laid out flat. The maps in this book use projections like this.

TYPES OF MAP

Different types of map can show different types of information. Physical maps show physical features, such as mountains and rivers, while political maps show countries and cities. Schematic maps show specific types of information, such as routes on an underground train network, and they may not necessarily show things in exactly the right place.

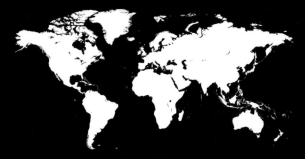

Physical map

Political map

Schematic map

Coloured regions

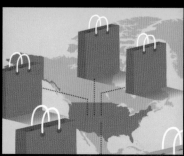

Scaled symbols

MAP SYMBOLS

Maps use lots of symbols to show information, such as blue lines for rivers and colours for different regions. Some of the symbols in this book show the locations of subjects, or the symbols are different sizes to represent different values – the bigger the symbol, the greater the value.

GLOSSARY

CALORIE
A unit of energy our bodies get from food. The energy values of different foods are measured in calories. Specifically, a calorie is the amount of energy needed to raise the temperature of 1 g of water by 1°C.

CARNIVAL
An outdoor, public celebration that often takes place before the Christian season of Lent. Lent marks a period of fasting and prayer.

CIVILISATION
A society that has reached a high level of social development. For example, it may have invented sophisticated political, legal and writing systems, and created monumental art and architecture.

EMPIRE
A large territory, often including different cultures and peoples, that is united through conquest under the rule of one country.

FESTIVAL
A celebration often linked to a local community and its traditions.

Some festivals celebrate dates in the religious or farming calendars. Many festivals today are spectacular live music events.

GENDER
Male or female. The sex of a person or animal.

INVESTMENT
The money spent on something in the hope that it will provide future benefits or profits. For example, investing in education is thought to help improve a country's economic future.

MARKET
The trading of goods or services in different territories and industries. Usually, the level of supply and demand sets the price of the goods and services traded.

MINIMUM WAGE
The lowest wage an employer can legally pay a worker. Not all countries have a legal minimum wage.

OLYMPIC GAMES
The modern revival of ancient games once held at Olympus in

Greece. They are now held in summer and in winter, in a different country each time.

PILGRIMAGE
A journey with a spiritual meaning, for example to a place that is important to a person's religious faith, such as a shrine.

PUBLISHING
Making literature, information or music available to the public. This could be through printed books and magazines or through websites, downloads and streaming.

SOCIAL NETWORK
An online forum where users share thoughts, images and music with others.

STREAMING
An online stream of multimedia, such as music or a movie, that a user can receive without having to download it to a phone or a computer.

WEBSITES

WWW.NATIONALGEOGRAPHIC.COM/KIDS-WORLD-ATLAS/MAPS.HTML
The map section of the National Geographic website where readers can create their own maps and study maps covering different topics.

WWW.MAPSOFWORLD.COM/KIDS/
Website with a comprehensive collection of maps covering a wide range of themes that are aimed at students and available to download and print out.

HTTPS://WWW.CIA.GOV/LIBRARY/PUBLICATIONS/THE-WORLD-FACTBOOK/
The information resource for the Central Intelligence Agency (CIA), this offers detailed facts and figures on a range of topics, such as population and transport, about every single country in the world.

WWW.KIDS-WORLD-TRAVEL-GUIDE.COM
Website with facts and travel tips about a host of countries from around the world.

INDEX

A

architecture 6–7
authors 12, 13
Aztecs 5

B

baby names 8, 9
Bishwa Ijtema 22
Bollywood 21
books 12, 13
British empire 5

C

calories 10, 11
Caribana 23
carnivals 22, 23
cinemas 21
clothes 14, 15
Colosseum 7
cotton production 15

E, F

education 18, 19
Egypt 4
empires 4, 5
fashion 14, 15
fast food 11
festivals 22, 23
food and drink 10–11

football 24–25
Forbidden City 7

H, I, K

Hajj 22
Hollywood 20
Holy Roman Empire 4
Imperial China 4
Inca 5
Intruz 23
Karneval 23
Kumbh Mela 22

L, M

literacy 3
Machu Picchu 7
Mardi Gras 23
Maurya 4
Maya 5
Mongol empire 5
Mount Rushmore 7
movies 20, 21
music festivals 16, 17
music sales 16, 17

N

Nabataean 4
names 8–9
New Century Global Center 7
Nobel Prizes 18, 19
Nollywood 21

O, P

Olympic Games 26–27
Parthenon 7
Prambanan 7
publishing 12–13
pyramids 5, 7

R, S, T

religions 3
Russian empire 5
social media 3, 28–29
Spanish empire 5
St Basil's Cathedral 7
streaming 17
surnames 8, 9
Sydney Opera House 8
Taj Mahal 7
teachers 17

U, V, W

Umayyad Caliphate 5
vinyl records 17
World Youth Day 22

The publisher would like to thank the following for their kind permission to reproduce their photographs:

Key: (t) top; (c) centre; (b) bottom; (l) left; (r) right

Cover front, 1tc, 23cr istockphoto.com/luoman, Cover front, 1bl, 19cr shutterstock/Pe3k, 3 courtesy of NASA, Cover back, 6 istockphoto.com/sorbetto, istockphoto.com/Aaltazar, istockphoto.com/drmakkoy, shutterstock/Oktora, Decorwithme | Dreamstime.com, Cover front, 10, 11 istockphoto.com/Varijanta,

istockphoto.com/Askold Romanov, 8 noun project/Félix Péault, 16tl noun project/Parker Foote, 17t noun project/Maximillian Piras, 17bc noun project/Robert Salazar Jr., 23tl istockphoto.com/Joel Carillet, 23tr istockphoto.com/Ary6, 23tl istockphoto.com/MaestroBooks, 23tr istockphoto.com/jon11, 23lc istockphoto.com/tamara_kulikova, 23c istockphoto.com/TimEKlein 23 cb istockphoto.com/deadandliving, 23 br istockphoto.com/bukharova, 25br Dreamstime.com/Taronin, 28bc noun project/Creative Stall PK